Many Ideas Open The Way

A Collection of Hmong Proverbs

Photographic Illustration by
Randy Snook

SHEN'S
BOOKS
Fremont,
California

To my wife, Sue, and my children, Lauren, Brian and Sara.

Library of Congress Cataloging-in-Publication Data

Snook, Randy.
Many ideas open the way : a collection of Hmong proverbs / collection
and photographs by Randy Snook.
p. cm.
Hmong and English.
Summary: A collection of twenty proverbs from the Hmong tradition, such
as "The mouth tastes food; the heart tastes words," which represent the
culture and heritage of this South Asian people.
1. Proverbs, Hmong--Translations into English--Juvenile literature.
2. Proverbs, Hmong--Juvenile literature. [1. Proverbs, Hmong. 2. Hmong
language materials--Bilingual.] I. Title.
PN6377.H54S66 2003   398.9'9572--dc21   2002153937

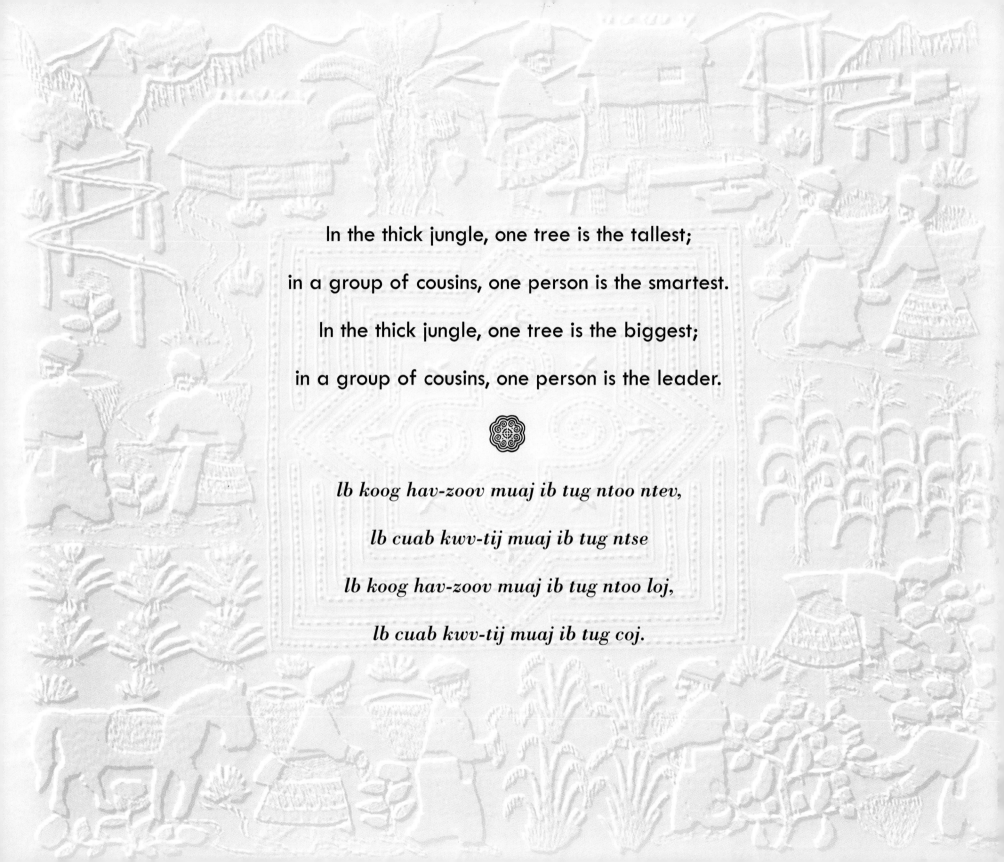

In the thick jungle, one tree is the tallest;

in a group of cousins, one person is the smartest.

In the thick jungle, one tree is the biggest;

in a group of cousins, one person is the leader.

lb koog hav-zoov muaj ib tug ntoo ntev,

lb cuab kwv-tij muaj ib tug ntse

lb koog hav-zoov muaj ib tug ntoo loj,

lb cuab kwv-tij muaj ib tug coj.

Fish will follow the river;

no rivers ever follow the fish.

Tsuas muaj tus ntses lawv tus dej

Tsis muaj tus dej lawv tus ntses

Whether you eat or not, at least hold a spoon;
whether you laugh or not, at least smile.

Noj tsis noj kuj tuav diav. Luag tsis luag kuj ntxi hniav.

Many hands make light work,
many ideas open the way.

Ntau txhais tes ua hauj-lwm sib, ntau lub tswv-yim ua tau txoj kev qhib.

Think before you speak,

translate before you explain.

Xav tau mam li hais

Txhais tau mam li cais.

When crossing a river, you shed your shoes;

flee from your country and you will lose your status.

Hla dej yuav hle khau

Tsiv-teb -tsaws-chaw yuav hle hau

Those who live far away love one another;
those that live close together dislike one another.

Nyob deb sib hlub, nyob ze sib ntxub.

Tangled hair: use a comb to unsnarl it.
Complicated dispute: ask an elder to solve it.

Plaub-hau ntxhov thiaj yuav zuag los ntsis; plaub ntug ntxhov thiaj yuav txwj laus los lis.

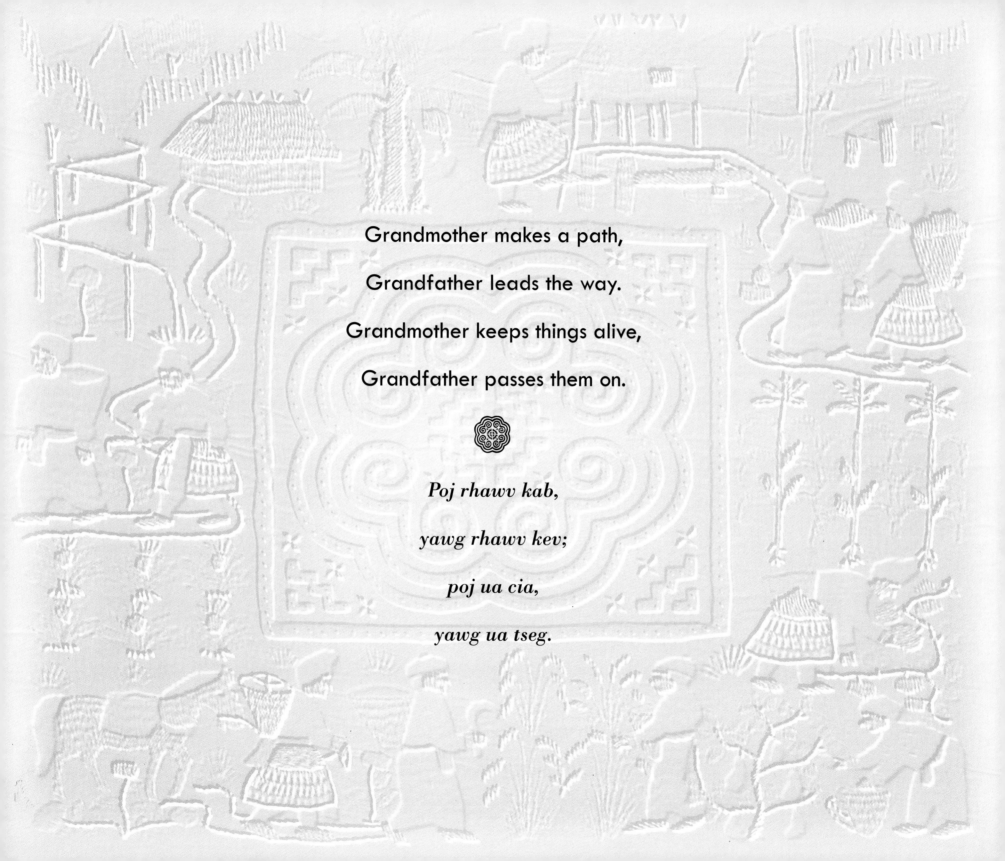

Grandmother makes a path,

Grandfather leads the way.

Grandmother keeps things alive,

Grandfather passes them on.

Poj rhawv kab,

yawg rhawv kev;

poj ua cia,

yawg ua tseg.

The mouth tastes food; the heart tastes words.

Qav muag ncauj; lus muag siab.

Parents are the sky, children are the earth.

Niam-txiv piv tam lub ntuj; tub-ki piv tam daim av.

If an orphaned calf survives, it may become an ox.

If an orphaned boy survives, he may become a village elder.

If an orphaned chick survives, it may become a rooster.

If an orphaned boy survives, he may become a village leader.

Nyuj ntsuag tsis tuag, nyuj ntsuag hlob tiav pwj

Tub ntsuag tsis tuag, tub ntsuag hlob ciaj xeev txwj

Qaib ntsuag tsis tuag, qaib ntsuag hlob tiav lau

Tub ntsuag tsis tuag, tub ntsuag hlob ciaj hau.

See a tiger and you will die;

see a government official and you will be poor.

Pom tsov yuav tuag

Pom nom-tswv yuav pluag.

If you heed your parents' advice when young,
you will become the village chief when grown.

Mloog niam txiv qhuab qhia thaum yau, loj hlob lo thiaj tau ua hau.

There is no need to sharpen a thorn;
there is no need to explain things to a smart person.

Pos ntse tsis yuav hliav, neeg ntse tsis yuav piav.

The wind always strikes the highest mountain.

Cua tuaj yeej xub raug lab roob siab.

A cow cannot see the skin of its chin;
a person cannot see his own face.

Nyuj tsis pom nyuj ntab, neeg tsis pom neeg hiab-xab.

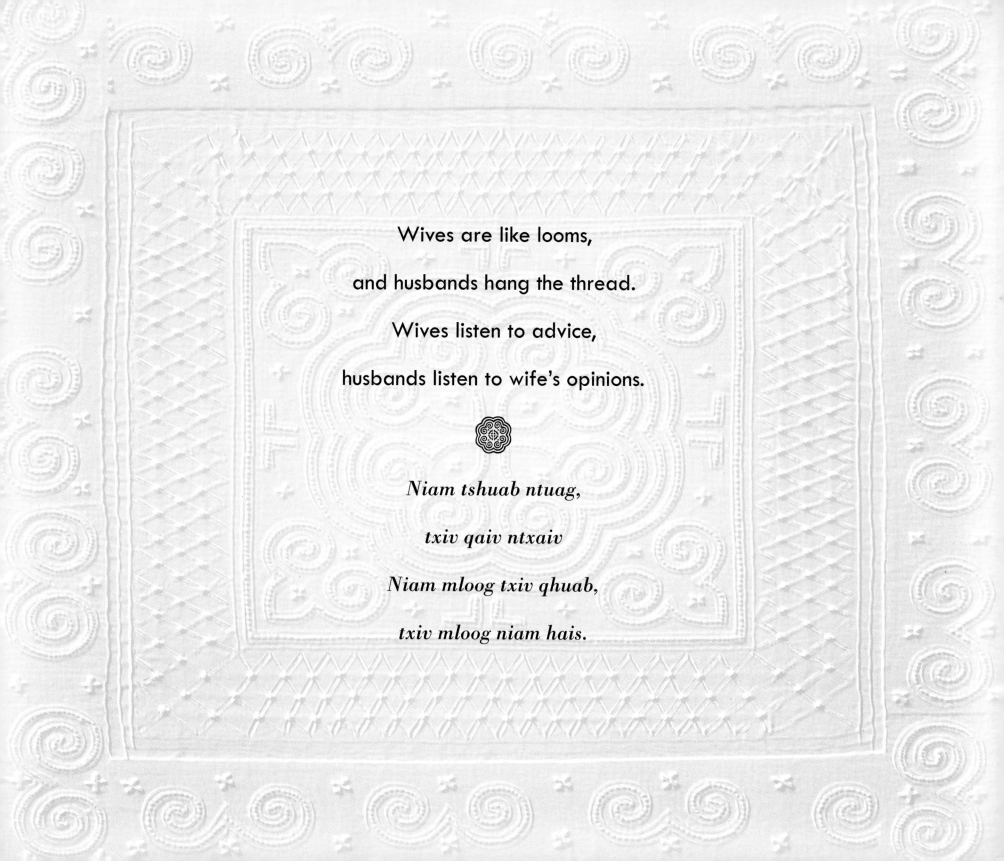

Wives are like looms,

and husbands hang the thread.

Wives listen to advice,

husbands listen to wife's opinions.

Niam tshuab ntuag,

txiv qaiv ntxaiv

Niam mloog txiv qhuab,

txiv mloog niam hais.

Old cows have crooked horns,

old bachelors have creaky voices.

Old trees have many dry twigs,

old people are still very young at heart.

Nyuj laus nyuj kub kawb

Nraug laus nraug suab hawb

Ntoo laus ntoo yoog kav

Neeg laus lawm los tseem xav xav.

The blind can see the road in the dim moonlight,

the deaf can hear a whisper.

The blind can see things in the road at night,

the deaf can hear something scratching the dried hide of a cow.

Dig-muag pom kev nruab qaig-hli

Lag-ntseg hnov lus ntxhi

Dig-muag pom kev yam hmo-ntuj

Lag-ntseg hnov kes tawv nyuj.

Artist's Note

To understand the proverbs of the Hmong, you must first understand something of their culture and the nature of proverbs. The Hmong are believed to have been a distinct cultural group for at least 4,000 years. Though they originally lived in what is now modern day China, the Hmong have often been forced to move in order to escape persecution and to avoid being governed or controlled by other people's and their governments. Theirs is a society with its own structure that does not desire or easily accept the rule of others. The Hmong are a society of great beauty and strength. Their beauty can be seen in their elaborate and ornate clothing, embroidery and other crafts. Throughout hundreds of years of persecution by many groups, the Hmong have remained a strong and vibrant society. To remain independent they have lived as farmers in the highlands of Southeast Asia. By working diligently they have not only survived, but flourished. Because the Hmong chose to fight against the communists in Southeast Asia during the Vietnam War, they came under great persecution when the communists took over. This persecution has forced them to leave their homeland once again.

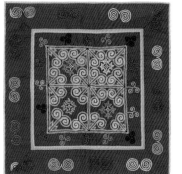

They have come to live in the United States, France, Germany, Australia, Canada and a host of other nations. But one thing has not changed, they are still the Hmong. They remain a people who love their children, respect their elders, believe in hard work and helping one another. They are a truly amazing and resilient culture that we can all learn from. These proverbs contain a small portion of the wisdom of the Hmong. As you read them you will find that many of the proverbs contain universal truths. When studying Hmong proverbs, or the proverbs from any culture, one thing you will hopefully discover is that while we are all unique, we are also all very much the same.

Clans

The Hmong identify themselves by what clan they belong to. These clan names are used as a surname in the United States, though it would have come first in their homeland. The major clans include the Chas, the Chengs, the Chues, the Fangs, the Hangs, the Hers, the Hues, the Kongs, the Kues, the Lees, the Los, the Mouas, the Phas, the Thaos, the Vangs, the Vues, the Xiongs and the Yangs. Women traditionally keep their clan name after marrying, while children take on the clan name of their father.

Special Thanks

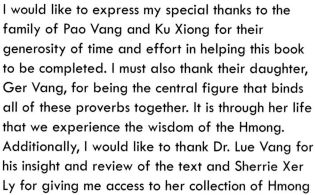

I would like to express my special thanks to the family of Pao Vang and Ku Xiong for their generosity of time and effort in helping this book to be completed. I must also thank their daughter, Ger Vang, for being the central figure that binds all of these proverbs together. It is through her life that we experience the wisdom of the Hmong. Additionally, I would like to thank Dr. Lue Vang for his insight and review of the text and Sherrie Xer Ly for giving me access to her collection of Hmong needleworks. Finally, I would like to thank BJ Ueltzen, my son Brian and my daughter Lauren who assisted me with the photography.

Photographic Illustrations copyright ©2003 by Randy Snook
Book Design by Randy Snook
Printed in Hong Kong • All rights reserved
No part of this book may be used or reproduced in any form or by any means, mechanical or electronic, without permission in writing from the publisher.

Shen's Books
40951 Fremont Blvd. • Fremont, CA 94538
1-800-456-6660 • www.shens.com